P9-AOT-171

SNAPSHOTS IN HISTORY

THE IRAN-CONTRA AFFAIR

Political Scandal Uncovered

by Lisa Klobuchar

THE IRAN-CONTRA AFFAIR

Political Scandal Uncovered

by Lisa Klobuchar

Content Adviser: Everett J. Carter, Ph.D.,
Assistant Professor of History, Pacific University

Reading Adviser: Susan Kesselring, M.A., Literacy Educator,
Rosemount-Apple Valley-Eagan (Minnesota) School District

Compass Point Books ✦ Minneapolis, Minnesota

COMPASS POINT BOOKS

3109 West 50th Street, #115
Minneapolis, MN 55410

 This book was manufactured with paper containing
at least 10 percent post-consumer waste.

For Compass Point Books
Brenda Haugen, XNR Productions, Inc., Catherine Neitge,
Keith Griffin, Lori Bye, and Nick Healy

Produced by White-Thomson Publishing Ltd.

For White-Thomson Publishing
Stephen White-Thomson, Susan Crean, Amy Sparks,
Tinstar Design Ltd., Kevin G. Cai, Peggy Bresnick Kendler,
Brian Fitzgerald, Barbara Bakowski, and Timothy Griffin

Library of Congress Cataloging-in-Publication Data
Klobuchar, Lisa.
  The Iran-Contra affair : political scandal uncovered / by Lisa Klobuchar.
    p. cm. — (Snapshots in history)
  Includes bibliographical references and index.
  ISBN 978-0-7565-3480-6 (library binding)
  1. Iran-Contra Affair, 1985–1990—Juvenile literature. 2. United
States—Foreign relations—1981–1989—Juvenile literature. 3. United
States—Politics and government—1981–1989—Juvenile literature.
4. Iran—Politics and government—1979–1997—Juvenile literature.
5. Nicaragua—Politics and government—1979–1990—Juvenile
literature. I. Title. II. Series.
  E876.K59 2008
  973.927—dc22   2007032700

Visit Compass Point Books on the Internet at
www.compasspointbooks.com
or e-mail your request to
custserv@compasspointbooks.com

CONTENTS

Crash in the Jungle

Chapter

1

On the morning of October 5, 1986, a C-123 cargo plane took off from an air base in the Central American country of El Salvador. Its mission was to deliver 5 tons (4.5 metric tons) of automatic rifles, ammunition, and combat boots to a rebel group called the Contras. The Contras were fighting the ruling Sandinista government in neighboring Nicaragua.

Of the plane's four-man crew, only the radio operator, Freddy Vilches, was a Contra. The others—pilot William Cooper, co-pilot Wallace "Buzz" Sawyer, and cargo handler Eugene Hasenfus—were Americans. All three men had experience in secret air operations for the U.S. military and the Central Intelligence Agency (CIA). But that day they were not entirely sure for whom they were working.

A Contra training camp in Honduras was one destination for American-supplied ammunition and weapons.

Meanwhile two Sandinista soldiers were watching for the flight. Contra supply planes had been spotted in the area several times in recent days. Now the Sandinistas were ready for another. They took up a position in the Nicaraguan jungle about 18 miles (28.8 kilometers) north of the city of San Carlos.

At 12:38 P.M. the Sandinistas heard the C-123 flying overhead. They fired a surface-to-air missile and scored a direct hit. As the plane tumbled into the jungle, a single parachute opened in the sky.

The next day, the Sandinistas found Eugene Hasenfus, the flight's sole survivor, hiding in an old hut on a nearby hilltop. By that evening, photos of his capture were broadcast around the world.

The sandy-haired 45-year-old was no stranger to secret supply missions. A former U.S. Marine, Hasenfus had served for six years as a supply specialist for Air America during the Vietnam War. Air America was an airline secretly owned and operated by the CIA. From 1962 until the end of the Vietnam War in 1975, Air America delivered supplies and transported troops and civilians, chiefly in Laos, Cambodia, and Vietnam.

In 1986, Hasenfus was a civilian living with his wife and three children in Wisconsin. He was employed as a construction worker when he received a call in June from pilot William Cooper, who had flown with Hasenfus for Air America. Cooper wanted to know if Hasenfus would be interested in making $3,000 a month for Corporate

Air Services. At that time, Cooper told Hasenfus that Corporate Air Services was a front company for the CIA and that the operation was being run "directly out of the White House."

American Eugene Hasenfus was captured in the Nicaraguan jungle.

11

Hasenfus accepted the offer. His position was known as the "kicker." He pushed the supplies out of the plane as it flew over drop sites. Cooper, Hasenfus, and the rest of the crew had made about 60 successful drops of supplies to the Contras before they were shot down. All the flights were dangerous. Daytime operations were risky but could not be avoided. The plane had no navigational equipment and could not fly at night. The C-123, flying low over the jungle in broad daylight, was an easy target.

Hasenfus quickly became a cooperative prisoner. The Sandinistas presented him at a news conference. Before the cameras, he freely admitted that he was part of a secret Contra supply operation. He said he believed the CIA ran it. This was only part of the full picture, however. Documents recovered at the crash site and telephone records uncovered by journalists shortly afterward pointed to an American operation that reached the highest levels of government.

A CHRISTMAS GIFT

The Sandinista government put Hasenfus on trial in Managua, the capital of Nicaragua. Although he had already publicly stated, "I'm guilty of everything they've charged," he pleaded not guilty on October 23 to the charges of terrorism, illicit association, and disrupting public security. He was convicted and sentenced to 30 years in prison. But Nicaraguan President Daniel Ortega made a goodwill gesture that he called "a Christmas message from the Nicaraguan people to the people of the United States." Ortega had Hasenfus released on December 17 and returned to the United States.

In Washington, D.C., several officials in President Ronald Reagan's administration denied having any involvement with Hasenfus or the downed flight. Within a week, Assistant Secretary of State Elliot Abrams denied U.S. responsibility for the incident to three congressional committees and on a national television program. Reagan himself told journalists that there was "no government connection with that [the Hasenfus flight] at all." Hasenfus' claims that the secret mission was run by the government were true, however, and the Reagan administration knew it.

As the fuss over the Contras raged in Washington, D.C., another scandal was unfolding half a world away. American agents were secretly trading arms to the government of Iran. In return, the Iranians offered to help arrange the release of American hostages held by Islamic militants in Lebanon. In a nationally televised speech on November 13, Reagan tried to put the nation's concerns over the Iran arms sales to rest. He said:

> *In spite of the wildly speculative and false stories of arms for hostages and alleged ransom payments, we did not—repeat did not—trade weapons or anything else for hostages, nor will we.*

But as new facts about the Iran and Contra operations surfaced, Americans began to doubt the honesty of the Reagan administration. Startling revelations followed soon after the speech. On

In November 1986, President Ronald Reagan assured the country that the U.S. government had not traded arms for hostages.

November 22, investigators discovered a document that described plans to send money from the Iranian arms sales to the Contras, far away in Central America. It was an explosive piece of evidence. Americans now were beginning to see how the

Reagan administration supported rebel groups and dealt with terrorists in ways that had been declared illegal by the U.S. Congress.

The Iran-Contra affair, as it came to be called, now dominated the news. In the months that followed, Americans listened to tales of secret, illegal arms sales and money transfers. Many were aghast at the lies, deceptions, and destruction of evidence that the major players used to cover up their wrongdoing. The affair grew into one of the biggest scandals in U.S. history. Before it was over, the Iran-Contra affair would divide the American people and cast a dark cloud over the nation's highest elected office. ◣

Secret Warriors

Chapter

2

In the early 1800s, the United States began to take a keen interest in the affairs of its Central American neighbors. The U.S. government feared that other world powers might try to suppress democracy in Central America. It seemed to people at the time that it was in the best interest of the United States to have democratic neighbors.

In 1823, President James Monroe issued a statement that said the United States would not tolerate any meddling by European countries in the Western Hemisphere. This statement became known as the Monroe Doctrine.

President Theodore Roosevelt extended the reach of the Monroe Doctrine in the early 1900s. He believed that troubles within Latin American countries might encourage European nations to interfere there. He believed that to prevent this, the United States had the right to preserve its power in the Western Hemisphere by using force, if necessary, to clear up trouble in Latin America.

In following Roosevelt's policy, the United States sent Marines into Nicaragua in 1912 to ensure that pro-U.S. leaders stayed in power. In 1927, long after Roosevelt left office, Cesar Augusto Sandino started a rebellion in Nicaragua to drive U.S. forces from the country. But the United States trained a Nicaraguan army, called the National Guard, to oppose him.

In 1933, General Anastasio Somoza Garcia became head of Nicaragua's National Guard. In February 1934, Somoza lured Sandino to a meeting, where Sandino was captured. The general had Sandino killed. Somoza took control of the Nicaraguan government on January 1, 1937, after a phony

Cesar Augusto Sandino opposed U.S. influence in Nicaragua in the early 1900s. He was murdered by General Anastasio Somoza's National Guard.

election. He ruled the country for the next 20 years, with the support of the U.S. government.

After World War II, the United States was the main trading partner of most Latin American countries. To protect its position, the United States provided a great deal of help in the form of economic aid to pro-American leaders. But an even graver threat than anti-U.S. leadership—at least in the eyes of the U.S. government—was on the rise. That threat was communism.

When World War II ended in 1945, the world's most powerful communist country was the Soviet Union. It wanted to spread communism— a political system in which property is owned by the government or community and profits are shared—wherever it could. As a result, the fear of communism influenced much of the foreign policy of the United States throughout the second half of the 20th century. U.S. involvement in the affairs of other nations was often an attempt to keep the Soviet Union in check.

In an address before Congress on March 12, 1947, President Harry S. Truman described the U.S. position on communism. In what became known as the Truman Doctrine, the president said that freedom was every human being's right. He said:

I believe that it must be the policy of the United States to support free peoples who are

President Harry S. Truman signed the Foreign Aid Assistance Act, which aided Greece and Turkey and led to the establishment of the Truman Doctrine.

resisting attempted subjugation by armed minorities or by outside pressures. I believe that we must assist free peoples to work out their own destinies in their own way. I believe that our help should be primarily through economic and financial aid, which is essential to economic stability and orderly political processes.

The policy Truman declared became known as containment, and it was the central idea in the Truman Doctrine. Truman's speech marked the beginning of the Cold War, a period of more than 40 years of arms buildup and tension between the West and the Soviet Union and its communist allies.

Accurate information had been vital during World War II. Through spying, the Allies—including the United States, Great Britain, France, and the Soviet Union—were able to find out about their enemies' battle plans. After the war, the threat of spreading communism led to more secret activities. President Truman created several agencies to secretly gather information about foreign governments.

On July 26, 1947, President Truman signed the National Security Act into law. The act created the National Security Council (NSC) and the Central Intelligence Agency. The CIA, which is under the authority of the NSC, spies on other nations. The CIA also works to influence events in other countries, mainly to help protect U.S. interests. Its main task during the Cold War was to stop the spread of communism. Much of the CIA's work was secret. The U.S. government did not publicly admit its role in secret operations—that is, unless its role in such operations was somehow uncovered.

THE NATIONAL SECURITY COUNCIL

The National Security Council is a group within the executive branch of government that advises the president on national security. The president serves as the chairman of the NSC. Other members are the vice president, the secretary of defense, and the secretary of state. In addition, the head of the Joint Chiefs of Staff and the director of the CIA act as advisers to the NSC. An official known as the assistant to the president for national security affairs directs the NSC staff. This person is usually called the national security adviser.

During the Cold War, the CIA secretly recorded Soviet communications and used spy planes and satellites to keep track of Soviet arms development and missile sites. It was CIA intelligence, for example, that informed the U.S. government about Soviet attempts to place nuclear missiles in Cuba. This discovery led to the Cuban missile crisis in the 1960s, which brought the United States and the Soviet Union dangerously close to a nuclear war.

Besides spying on the Soviets, the CIA took part in secret actions to influence the political direction foreign countries would take. Often the CIA helped groups in other countries remove socialist leaders. Similar to communists, socialists believe in a

The CIA gathered the intelligence that showed that the Soviets were placing missiles in Cuba.

MISSILE ERECTOR

CABLE

MISSILE SHELTER TENT

TRACKED PRIME MOVERS

OXIDIZER TANK TRAILERS

TRAILERS

21

greater government role in controlling businesses within a country. Their main goal is to ensure that wealth and power are shared equally among all citizens, rich and poor. Usually the United States viewed socialists as dangerous to U.S. interests. In 1954, the CIA helped military forces in Guatemala overthrow a socialist government that had been freely elected.

The CIA had unsuccessful secret operations as well. One failed CIA operation was an attempt to overthrow Cuban dictator Fidel Castro in 1961, in what became known as the Bay of Pigs invasion. In 1959, Castro had taken power in Cuba, an island nation only 90 miles (144 km) from the state of Florida. Castro took power by overthrowing the U.S.-supported dictator Fulgencio Batista. Under Batista, the United States wielded much influence in Cuba, and U.S. businesses made big profits there.

THE BAY OF PIGS INVASION

On April 15, 1961, Cubans flying U.S. aircraft bombed air bases in Cuba. On April 17, more American-backed Cuban forces came ashore at several places on the island. The main landing site was the Bay of Pigs, on the southern coast. Cuban leader Fidel Castro's forces quickly defeated the invaders, killing about 200 and imprisoning about 1,100. In December 1962, the United States gave Cuba about $53 million worth of food and medicine—collected from private donors—in exchange for the release of the prisoners.

In a top-secret analysis of the mission, completed six months later, the CIA was critical of its own performance in the operation. The report made it clear that the CIA knew in advance that the mission would most likely fail. It withheld that information from the president to ensure that the mission would go forward. Then the administration and the CIA feared that if Congress and the public found out about the deception, they might demand that the CIA not be allowed to carry on secret operations. The report was kept secret and not released to the public until 1998.

Eventually Congress became fed up with unchecked CIA activities. In 1974, Congress passed a law requiring the president to inform Congress in writing that any planned secret CIA operation was "important to the national security of the United States." Such reports, known as findings, were to describe what type of operation was being planned and why it was necessary.

In 1980, Congress passed another law that required the president to inform the special intelligence committees in the U.S. Senate and House of any spying activities in advance. But the CIA and the White House did not always play by the rules. ◣

Two Revolutions

From all outward appearances, the nations of Iran and Nicaragua could not be more different. Iran is an oil-rich desert country on the Arabian Peninsula in Asia with a Muslim tradition. Nicaragua is a poor tropical nation in Central America. But at the beginning of 1979, the two countries did have one important thing in common: The United States and its allies supported them and had helped put their rulers in place.

The United States had been involved in the affairs of Iran since World War II. During the war, Iran's ruler, Reza Shah Pahlavi, expanded trade with Nazi Germany. He also tried to prevent the Allies from transporting war supplies to the Soviet Union through Iran. To keep the supply lines open, the Soviet Union and Great Britain

invaded Iran. They removed Reza Shah from power and on September 16, 1941, replaced him with his eldest son, Mohammed Reza Shah Pahlavi.

Mohammed Reza, like his father, was a secular, or nonreligious, ruler. He was known as the shah of Iran. During the first decade of his rule, the new shah struggled against various political parties, trade unions, religious leaders, and foreign governments

Reza Shah Pahlavi (right) became ruler of Iran in 1925 and was replaced by his eldest son, Mohammed Reza Shah Pahlavi, in 1941.

25

to hold power. Mohammed Reza Shah was a weaker ruler than his father had been. He was vulnerable to challenges from the elected Iranian parliament, known as the Majlis.

After the war, the shah maintained close and friendly relations with Western powers, including the United States. Both the shah and the United States were committed to resisting the Soviets, and the United States rewarded the shah for his loyalty by providing generous economic and military aid to Iran.

The United States wanted to maintain a friendly relationship with Iran.

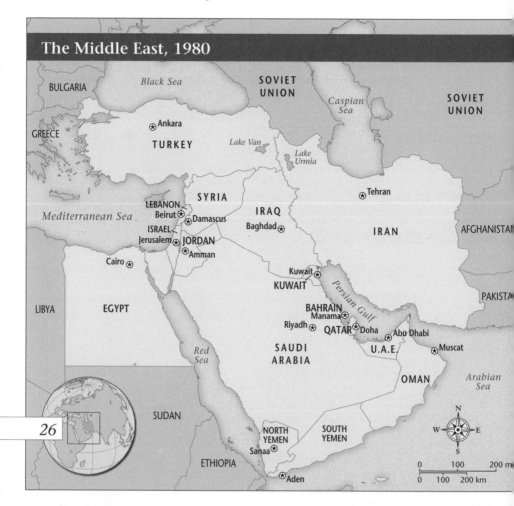

The Middle East, 1980

In order to maintain these friendly relations, the United States did all it could to ensure that the shah remained in power. In 1953, a popular prime minister named Mohammad Mosaddeq threatened the shah's position. As prime minister of Iran, Mosaddeq had imposed state control on the oil industry.

Mosaddeq was widely supported by the Iranian people. When the shah tried to remove him from office, widespread protests in August 1953 forced the shah to flee the country. The United States wasted no time in reversing the situation. The CIA provided money and aid to Mosaddeq's opponents, and the shah was returned to power less than a week later.

With steady U.S. support, the shah ruled Iran for the next 25 years. He used money from the oil industry to make many improvements to Iranian life. He expanded transportation and irrigation, improved health services and education, and broadened the rights of women. He also undertook a program of land reform in which land was taken from *ulama,* or elite religious leaders, and given to farmers.

OIL IN IRAN

The oil industry had been significant in Iran since the 1920s. Since the early 1900s, it had been controlled by a British company called the Anglo-Persian Oil Company. Like his father before him, Mohammed Reza Shah Pahlavi tolerated Great Britain's control of oil production. This became a point of great irritation among some Iranians. When Mohammad Mosaddeq nationalized the oil industry, the British responded by slapping economic embargoes on Iran. The oil industry weakened under state control, and the country suffered economically.

Under the shah, however, Iranians had limited freedom, the government was corrupt, and the gap between the wealthy and the poor was vast. The SAVAK, a secret police force founded and trained with the help of the CIA, spread fear and put down any attempts to oppose the shah's rule, often with torture.

The shah's close relationship with the United States helped him maintain control until the late 1970s. The U.S. Embassy in Iran's capital city, Tehran, had a large staff of more than 1,400 people. American advisers influenced economic policies. American experts also played a key role in developing the Iranian army into one of the largest, best-equipped, highly trained fighting forces in the world. The shah helped make the army even stronger by buying about $4 billion worth of weapons from the United States every year.

But not all Iranians approved of the shah's policies. One of the shah's most influential critics was Ruhollah Khomeini, an ayatollah, or Muslim religious leader. Khomeini had been exiled, or forced to leave the country, because of his antigovernment stance. He spent most of his exile in Iraq. In the 1970s, Khomeini's ideas spurred students, poor people, the Muslim clergy, and small-business owners to action. Widespread demonstrations, strikes, and other forms of protest broke out in 1978.

Government forces tried to stop the protests, and many people were killed. Khomeini oversaw the chaos from exile. On January 16, 1979, the shah was forced from power and fled the country. On February 1, Khomeini arrived in Tehran and took control of the government.

On April 1, Khomeini declared Iran an Islamic republic. He replaced nonreligious government officials with Muslim clerics. He also stripped women of rights they had gained under the shah's regime and banned alcohol and Western

An Air France jet returned Ayatollah Ruhollah Khomeini to Tehran on February 1, 1979, after 15 years of exile.

29

KHOMEINI'S CRITICISMS

In the early 1960s, Ruhollah Khomeini began speaking out against Mohammed Reza Shah's pro-Western policies and secular reforms. Khomeini was against reforms that took land and power from clerics (religious leaders). He opposed increasing women's rights and freedom. He also criticized secular influences in schools and courts. Khomeini spent a year in prison for his antigovernment activities. After his release he was exiled, on November 4, 1964. Throughout his exile, he communicated with Iranians by means of speeches and sermons smuggled into the country in print and on audiotape. He called for the shah to step down.

music. He formed his own secret police to enforce his conservative Islamic policies. The United States maintained its embassy but cut the staff to about 70 people. Less extreme members of Iran's new government tried to protect what was left of the embassy.

Ill with cancer, the shah eventually fled to the United States. Young Khomeini supporters— mostly students—angrily protested at the U.S. Embassy in Tehran. They demanded the return of the shah to Iran to face trial for his wrongdoing. On November 4, 1979, about 3,000 students seized the embassy, taking 66 employees at the embassy hostage. The U.S. government refused to turn the shah over. President Jimmy Carter first used diplomatic means to try to secure the release of the hostages. When that failed, he ordered an embargo of Iranian oil and then extended it to other goods. Still the hostages remained in captivity.

The situation damaged U.S. prestige around the world. Adding to the region's problems—and Carter's troubles—the Soviet Union invaded Afghanistan on December 24, 1979. Presidential elections were scheduled for the following November, and the situation was endangering Carter's chances for re-election.

Diplomacy and the embargo clearly were not working. Carter increased pressure on Iran by cutting off diplomatic relations on April 8, 1980. Dramatic action was now called for. It came in the form of a daring and complicated rescue mission that had been in the planning stages for several months. It was code-named Operation Eagle Claw.

Iranian students seized the U.S. Embassy in Tehran on November 4, 1979, and took dozens of hostages. Days later, the hostage takers displayed a bound and blindfolded American hostage to reporters and photographers.

President Carter gave final approval for Operation Eagle Claw on April 16, 1980. Three days later, the mission was launched. Eight Navy helicopters took off from the aircraft carrier USS *Nimitz* in the Persian Gulf near the coast of Iran. Immediately after, six transport planes carrying supplies and more fuel for the helicopters departed from Masirah Island, off the coast of Oman.

The plan was for them to meet at a refueling area in the desert. Then they would fly to the outskirts of Tehran before continuing by ground to the embassy. Commandos would storm the embassy, rescue the hostages, and then escape by helicopter.

But the mission was in trouble from the start. One of the helicopters broke down, and the other pilots encountered dust storms. Then another helicopter broke down at the staging area. Because of the difficulties, organizers decided to cancel the mission. On the way back to the *Nimitz,* one of the helicopters collided with one of the refueling planes, destroying both and killing eight members of the mission. Seven helicopters and the bodies of the eight dead Americans were abandoned in the desert. Before television cameras, Iranian officials displayed the bodies of the eight servicemen killed in the crash.

Mohammed Reza Shah died in Cairo, Egypt, on July 27, 1980. Soon after, Iraq invaded Iran. Eight years of war between the two countries followed.

Combined with the pressures of war, the embargoes against Iran became even more damaging to the country's economy and the standard of living of its people. Many nations withheld aid from Iran as long as the country continued to hold the hostages. Iran agreed to resume negotiations, and the U.S. government agreed to release Iranian money seized in the United States and lift trade penalties. But the hostages remained in custody.

Partly as a result of the ongoing hostage crisis and the disastrous rescue attempt, Carter lost his re-election bid. Instead American voters elected Republican Ronald Reagan as their new president in November 1980.

At about the same time, another revolution was taking place, this one in Nicaragua. The United States was deeply interested in events in Latin America because U.S. businesses had invested a lot of money in the region. The United States also wanted to ensure that governments friendly to U.S. interests stayed in power.

The communist-led Sandinista National Liberation Front had been formed to oppose the regime of Anastasio Somoza Debayle, whose family had ruled Nicaragua

THE SOMOZA REGIME

When General Anastasio Somoza Garcia was assassinated on September 21, 1956, his oldest son, Luis Somoza Debayle, assumed the presidency of Nicaragua. He left office in 1963. Somoza allies ran the government until 1967, when Luis died and his younger brother, Anastasio Somoza Debayle, became president. The Somozas were strong rulers, and the political situation was stable while they were in power. U.S. businesses invested profitably in Nicaragua, so the U.S. government supported the Somoza regime. The Somoza family mainly used its power to enrich itself and its allies.

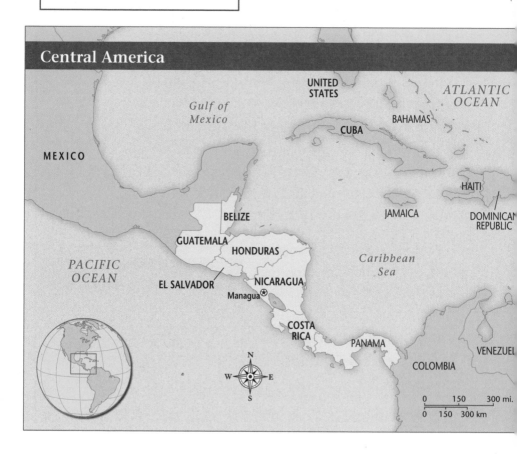

Central America

Nicaragua's nearness to Cuba fueled fears that it would become friendly with communist regimes.

for years. The group was named after the rebel leader Cesar Augusto Sandino, who had been killed by the Somoza regime in 1934. In the mid-1970s, the Sandinistas and another opposition group began a campaign to remove the Somoza regime from power. Thousands of civilians were killed during several years of disorder.

In 1978, the conflict became a full-blown civil war. The Sandinistas and their allies, which now included the Roman Catholic Church, had the support of many civilians. During the next 18 months, they were able to take control of much of the country.

On July 17, 1979, Somoza resigned and fled to the United States.

The Sandinistas set up a new government and seized property owned by the Somoza family and its supporters. They also took control of important parts of the economy, including banking, insurance, mining, and forestry. They began to establish ties with communist nations such as Cuba and the Soviet Union.

The Democratic Carter administration wanted to keep relations with the Sandinista regime as friendly as possible in the hope of keeping it from getting too friendly with Cuba and the Soviet Union. So in 1979 and 1980, the United States sent $99 million in emergency food and economic aid to Nicaragua. President Reagan and the Republicans, however, felt differently from the Democrats about the Sandinistas. Reagan was determined to keep his campaign promise that the U.S. government would do all it could to help the opponents of the Sandinistas in Nicaragua set up a new government. ◣

Reagan vs. Congress

Chapter

4

Ronald Reagan took office as the 40th U.S. president in January 1981. He was a strong opponent of communism. His tough policies toward the Soviet Union would later be given credit for ending the Cold War in the early 1990s.

In the case of Iran-Contra, however, his efforts to combat communism led him into scandal. But Reagan had a unique ability to come out of such situations with little damage to his reputation or popularity. This quality earned Reagan the nickname the "Teflon president" because nothing stuck to him.

By the time Reagan took office, the Sandinista government had signed agreements with the Soviet Union to trade, share scientific knowledge,

and learn about each other's arts and ways of life. Cuba had sent advisers to Nicaragua. The Sandinistas also supplied arms to socialist rebels in El Salvador. The Reagan administration viewed this as a sign of growing communist influence in the Western Hemisphere.

Ronald Reagan was sworn into office on January 20, 1981.

As a result, in February 1981, the United States cut off economic aid to Nicaragua. On November 17, Reagan authorized a program of secret support for the anti-Sandinistas. The administration publicly revealed only that it would help block arms shipments from Nicaragua to El Salvador.

Anti-Sandinista forces had begun to form in Honduras and Costa Rica. The CIA decided to back a group called the Fuerza Democrática Nicaragüense (FDN), or the Nicaraguan Democratic Force. The FDN was made up of former officers of the Nicaraguan National Guard—Somoza's army— who were based in Honduras. Throughout 1982, the CIA secretly provided training to the FDN. Another group, the Frente Sandinista de Liberación Nacional (FSLN), or Sandinista Revolutionary Front, was made up of disgruntled Sandinistas based in Costa Rica. Together these groups became known as the Contras.

Contra fighters resisted the Sandinista government in Nicaragua beginning in 1979. In 1981, the newly elected U.S. president, Ronald Reagan, began to equip them with supplies, weapons, and other forms of support.

The secret activities in which the U.S. government was involved were soon made public, and the reaction was not positive. The November 8, 1982, issue of *Newsweek* magazine had a cover story called "America's Secret War: Nicaragua" that was based in part on an interview with CIA Director William Casey. The article suggested that the U.S. government was involved in an effort to overthrow Nicaragua's Sandinista government.

The *Boston Globe* responded to the *Newsweek* report by running an editorial on November 5, 1982, titled "Uncle Sam as Destabilizer." The editorial harshly criticized these activities. It asked:

> *Does America have the political right to impose a succession of military dictatorships and gangster governments on the sovereign peoples of Central America?*

Congressman Edward P. Boland, a Massachusetts Democrat, agreed with the *Boston Globe* that the answer was no. He chaired the House Select Committee on Intelligence, one of the congressional committees with the power to approve or prevent spying. But the Reagan administration had not sought such approval. On December 8, the House of Representatives—controlled by the Democrats—passed the bill authorizing the defense budget for 1983. Attached to that bill was an amendment addressing the issue of aid to the Contras.

The amendment, sponsored by Boland, made it illegal for the CIA and the Department of Defense to spend any money "for the purpose of overthrowing the government of Nicaragua or provoking a military exchange between Nicaragua and Honduras." Reagan signed the bill into law and promised to abide by the so-called Boland amendment. However, the CIA and the administration continued to explore ways to get around the Boland amendment by secretly moving aid to the Contras through other countries.

The Republican-controlled Senate wanted to continue aid to the Contras, and the Democratic-controlled House wanted to stop it entirely. In December 1983, the two houses of Congress agreed on a compromise. Congress would not stop support for the Contras outright, but it would limit funding to $24 million during the next year. This amount

Democratic Representative Edward P. Boland was against U.S. efforts to overthrow the Sandinistas.

probably would not last through the summer. But the Reagan administration did not waver in its determination to support the Contras. On May 3, 1983, Reagan declared that he supported "overt aid to the anti-Sandinista guerrillas [rebels] in Nicaragua."

At the same time, CIA officials and others in the executive branch were discussing placing mines, or hidden explosive devices, in three of Nicaragua's harbors. The purpose of the mines was to stop shipments of military supplies to the Sandinista government. The CIA worked closely with the NSC in planning and carrying out the mine placement. Among the government officials involved were National Security Adviser Robert C. McFarlane and Lieutenant Colonel Oliver L. North, a career marine officer and the NSC's chief action officer for Central American affairs.

President Reagan approved the plan, and the operation began on January 7, 1984. The mines were made in the United States, and an American ship under American command placed them. The operation was not a secret, but the CIA instructed the Contras to take responsibility. The mines damaged several ships.

The U.S. government's role in the operation became public as a result of an article in *The Wall Street Journal*. Members of the Senate Select Committee on Intelligence—another committee that by law was to be informed in advance of such operations—were furious. Senator Barry Goldwater, the Republican chairman of the committee, wrote a scathing letter to CIA Director William Casey when the news became public. The letter said, in part:

> *Dear Bill:*
>
> *All this past weekend, I've been trying to figure out how I can most easily tell you my feelings about the discovery of the President having approved mining some of the harbors of Central America.*
>
> *It gets down to one, little, simple phrase:*
>
> *I am [very angry]! ...*
>
> *I am forced to apologize to the members of the Intelligence Committee because I did not know the facts on this. At the same time, my counterpart in the House did know.*
>
> *The President has asked us to back his foreign policy ...*
>
> *The deed has been done and, in the future, if anything like this happens, I'm going to raise ... a lot of fuss about it in public.*
>
> *Sincerely,*
>
> *Barry Goldwater, Chairman*

Casey defended the mine placement by claiming that he had informed the committee about the operation in March. But Casey had told the committee only that mines had been placed in the harbors, not that the CIA had planted them—nor had he informed the committee in advance. The Senate demanded more say in the carrying out of secret operations. From then on, the CIA would be required to turn over to the Senate intelligence committee any presidential findings on secret activities and any plans for secret operations in advance.

The U.S. Congress thought that the Boland amendment would settle the Contra matter. What it didn't know was how deeply involved with the Contras the U.S. government already was. ◣

BOLAND II

The mine placement led to passage of another Boland amendment on October 12, 1984. Boland II was intended to close any loopholes left open by the first Boland amendment. It prohibited any form of support from any intelligence agency of the U.S. government for any activity aimed against the Nicaraguan government.

Aiding the Contras "Body and Soul"

The mine-setting incident's immediate effect was to sour Congress on resuming aid to the Contras. The Reagan administration knew this. Reagan and his supporters, however, were willing and able to be creative—and even sneaky—in order to keep aid flowing to the Contras.

In early 1984, the Reagan administration was carrying out its Contra policies with the belief that it could get around the Boland amendments in two ways. First, it could deliver aid to the Contras through the NSC. As the administration saw it, the NSC wasn't directly involved in spying. If the Boland amendments applied only to spy agencies, then it was not a violation of law to use the NSC to aid the Contras. Second, the administration could aid the Contras with funds raised from either private individuals or from other countries.

This line of thinking was how Oliver North, who had no previous experience in spying activities, ended up in the middle of one of the most notorious secret operations in U.S. history.

With the blessing of the Reagan administration—and very little supervision—Lieutenant Colonel Oliver "Ollie" North carried out the Iran-Contra operation.

North had joined the NSC on August 4, 1981. His first assignment was to help with the sale of sophisticated radar surveillance planes to Saudi Arabia. After this assignment, he worked on several low-profile projects. His boss was Robert McFarlane, the deputy national security adviser. A former Marine, McFarlane thought highly of North's performance and began to give him more important assignments. One of these was to serve on a commission that helped develop U.S. policy on Central America. This work made North well versed on Central American affairs.

North's ability to carry out complex tasks efficiently—as well as his dedication to Reagan's Nicaraguan policy—made him the perfect person to head the secret Contra aid program. North would get input from CIA Director William Casey. Then Casey could claim he had no direct involvement in the activities. In this way, the Reagan administration believed that it could avoid violating the Boland amendments.

To keep the rest of the Reagan administration as distant as possible from the support of the Contras, the NSC and CIA allowed Oliver North absolute freedom to carry out the operation. North soon became practically a one-man operation within the government. He carried out time-consuming and complex tasks—from fundraising to advising and caring for the Contra leaders—efficiently and skillfully.

On January 6, 1984, the National Security Planning Group (NSPG) directed McFarlane, who had been promoted to national security adviser, to raise $10 million to $15 million in additional aid. Reagan had formed the NSPG in 1981 to sort out difficulties in coordinating the various departments involved in foreign policy. The NSPG included some of the highest-ranking officials in the United States, including the president, vice president, secretaries of state and defense, and national security adviser.

The Contras needed supplies to maintain patrols around Nicaragua.

47

Contra fighters relaxed at a base camp.

In May 1984, McFarlane received a pledge from the Saudi Arabian government of $1 million a month until the end of the year for the Contras. McFarlane got the number of a Contra bank account from North and passed it along to the Saudis. The Saudis deposited the money directly into the Contra account. McFarlane reported the donation to President Reagan, telling him, "No one knows about this." According to McFarlane, the president replied, "Good. Let's just make sure it stays that way."

By this time, the president's intentions with regard to the Contras were more than clear. According to McFarlane, Reagan said during the spring or summer of 1984 that he wanted the Contras to stay together and keep fighting. McFarlane said:

> *He let us know very clearly ... that we were to do all that we could to make sure that the movement, the freedom fighters [Contras], survived and I think the term at the time that's come up here and there was that we were to do all we could to keep them together "body and soul."*

Throughout the next two years, North, Reagan, McFarlane, and other administration officials continued to seek funds not only from foreign governments but also from private U.S. donors. President Reagan supported these activities by occasionally attending private meetings at which North explained to potential donors the need for such funds. Donors were often rewarded by being photographed with the president.

With a new source of funding, North and the others now needed someone to supply the Contras with weapons. This job fell to retired Air Force Major General Richard V. Secord. Casey recommended Secord to North for two main reasons. Secord had a lot of experience in secret operations, and he had contacts within the international arms trade. In the summer of 1984, North asked Secord to help the Contras buy weapons.

One of Secord's acquaintances was an Iranian-born American businessman named Albert Hakim. Secord and Hakim started putting together weapons deals for the Contras. They bought arms, which they then sold to the Contras for a profit, eventually earning them millions of dollars. Secord and Hakim called their operation "the Enterprise."

The Enterprise arranged the first shipments of arms to the Contras in November 1984. It used a Canadian arms dealer called Transworld Armament to arrange for weapons manufactured in East Asia and Europe to be delivered to the Contras by sea

Enterprise-supplied weapons fueled the Contra fight against Sandinistas in Nicaragua.

and air. A Cuban named Rafael Quintero, who had previously worked for the CIA, became the Enterprise's go-between in Central America. He made sure that the arms were delivered to the Contra forces.

North also gave information to the Contras to help them fight the Sandinistas. That November, Contra leaders asked North for information on where the Sandinistas were keeping Soviet-supplied military helicopters. North got the information from contacts in the U.S. military and the CIA. North's contacts did not know he was passing the information on to the Contras.

North put the Contras in touch with the British, who worked with them on plans to destroy the helicopters. But the British considered the operation too dangerous and did not go through with it. They did, however, blow up a Sandinista weapons storage facility in Managua, Nicaragua's capital city, on March 6, 1985.

With money provided by North, the Contras began to work with other arms dealers besides the Enterprise. North saw that he was losing control of the Contras' operation and that its activities were becoming disorganized. The Contra forces in the north—the Nicaraguan Democratic Force—were doing most of the fighting. North wanted to get the Contra forces based in the south—the FSLN—to give the FDN more support. He needed to make sure the FSLN in the south was adequately supplied.

North informed Contra leaders at a meeting on June 28, 1985, in Miami that he would stop giving money directly to them. Instead, using money supplied by North, Secord would buy arms for the Contras. Secord also would take over the job of delivering them. The purpose was to turn the two separate Contra groups into a unified fighting force. In this way, North hoped they could increase pressure on the Sandinista government. Secord thus became the only arms dealer to the Contras.

The Enterprise soon owned airplanes and a ship, had its own airfield, and employed pilots and other staff. They communicated with North

Richard Secord used his experience in secret operations and in the international arms trade to carry out Contra supply missions.

and among themselves with sophisticated, secure communications devices supplied by the National Security Agency, which specializes in code-breaking. The Enterprise conducted its business with secret Swiss bank accounts. Now instead of the donations going directly to the Contras to use as they wished, funds meant for the Contras were deposited in the Enterprise's bank accounts.

In November 1985, the Enterprise set up an operation for airlifting weapons and other supplies to Contra forces in Guatemala and Nicaragua. The Enterprise used an airline called Southern Air Transport, based in Miami, to pick up weapons in Portugal. The planes then flew over Contra bases and used parachutes to drop the supplies. By mid-1986, the Enterprise was making regular, large supply deliveries from various sources to Contra forces throughout the region. ◣

Dealing With Iran

Chapter

6

Secret operations were not only taking place in Nicaragua. Across the globe in Iran, another secret arms deal was taking shape. At first these deals were separate from the Contra program. But the involvement of North and McFarlane soon brought the two operations together.

The Reagan administration disliked the Khomeini regime in Iran as much as it despised the Sandinistas in Nicaragua. After Iraq invaded Iran in September 1980, the United States had chosen to remain neutral in the war. But it also felt that an Iranian victory might threaten U.S. interests in the Persian Gulf region and endanger allies such as Saudi Arabia. So the United States began to provide Iraq with secret information about the Iranians. It also gave information to Iraq's allies in the Gulf region to protect them against a possible Iranian attack.

In March and April 1983, the United States began a campaign called Operation Staunch. Its aim was to persuade other countries not to sell arms to Iran. Iran had been a huge consumer of weapons,

War between Iran and Iraq broke out in 1980.

and more than 25 countries had been selling arms to it. U.S. State Department officials running Operation Staunch found many ways to stop the sale of weapons to Iran. They made personal visits to foreign countries and used friendly persuasion. They also lodged official protests.

If a country resisted, they even suggested that the United States might no longer authorize U.S. factories to manufacture U.S. weapons, planes, and other equipment. Operation Staunch was largely successful. Almost all U.S. allies stopped selling military equipment to Iran. The only countries still selling weapons to Iran were communist nations under the control of the Soviet Union.

An Islamic group released pictures in May 1985 of hostages it had kidnapped, including (from left) the Reverend Lawrence Jenco, CIA official William Buckley, and journalist Terry Anderson.

At the same time, the United States declared that Iran was a sponsor of international terrorism. It viewed the government in Iran as an active supporter of radical Islamic revolutionaries in other countries. In 1985, a radical Islamic group in Lebanon called Hezbollah was holding seven Americans hostage.

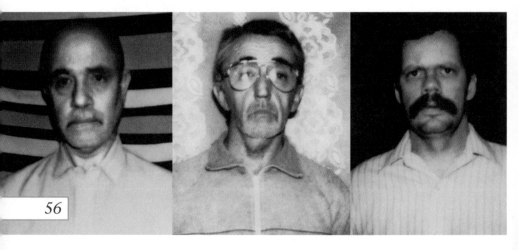

THE HOSTAGE TAKERS

Lebanon has had strong ties with the West since it became independent of French rule in 1943. Christians and Muslims shared power equally, and many Europeans and Americans worked in high-level positions in Lebanon. In 1958, Muslims rebelled. Full-blown civil war broke out in 1975. Various religious groups—Christians, Jews, Shiite Muslims, and Sunni Muslims—and their foreign allies fought against one another. In 1982, Iranian leader Ayatollah Khomeini sent a force of 1,000 Revolutionary Guards to train Lebanon's Shiite militia. The Iranians helped the Lebanese Shiites form Hezbollah, Arabic for "Party of God." The Shiite militia was soon fighting the Israelis, Christians, and Sunni Muslims. At the same time, U.S. Marines were stationed in Lebanon as part of an international peacekeeping force. Muslims in Lebanon viewed the Americans as foreign invaders. To protest this presence and to try to force the release of Muslim prisoners in Israel and elsewhere, Hezbollah began taking Westerners in Lebanon hostage.

The hostage takers were followers of the Shia branch of Islam. Since Shiites were the dominant Muslim sect in Iran, the United States believed that Iran could influence the hostage takers to release the American prisoners.

In public, at least, President Reagan was firm in his refusal to deal with Iran or negotiate with hostage takers. At a news conference on June 18, he stated his views:

> *Let me further make it plain to the assassins in Beirut and their accomplices, wherever they may be, that America will never make concessions to terrorists—to do so would only invite more terrorism—nor will we ask nor*

57

> *pressure any other government to do so. Once we head down that path there would be no end to it, no end to the suffering of innocent people, no end to the bloody ransom all civilized nations must pay.*

Behind the scenes, however, deals with Iran were in the making. The United States hoped that it could influence events in Iran. Its plan was to stay close to moderates in the government. American officials hoped that less extreme Iranians might not support Khomeini's radical Islamic government. The United States also felt it was important to reduce the threat of Soviet influence in Iran. In May 1985, a government intelligence report suggested the way to do this was to seek better relations with Iran. The report recommended that the U.S. government ease restrictions on arms sales to Iran. Secretary of State George Shultz and Secretary of Defense Caspar Weinberger disagreed with the recommendation. But CIA Director Casey and National Security Adviser McFarlane supported it.

NSC officials began discussing Iran with Israeli government officials. Israel shared the U.S. desire to improve relations with Iran, which had continued to buy arms from Israel. On July 3, 1985, McFarlane met with an Israeli foreign ministry official named David Kimche. He told McFarlane about Manucher Ghorbanifar, an Iranian businessman. Ghorbanifar claimed he was in contact with influential Iranians, including the prime minister.

These Iranians, Ghorbanifar said, would arrange for the release of the American hostages in Lebanon. In exchange, the United States would be required to provide 500 anti-tank, or TOW, missiles to Iran.

On July 16, President Reagan was recovering from surgery to remove a cancerous growth from his intestine. McFarlane visited the president in the hospital and told him about the proposal. The president gave McFarlane the go-ahead to explore it further. Early in August, McFarlane briefed President Reagan, Vice President George H.W. Bush, Secretary of Defense Weinberger, CIA Director Casey, and Secretary of State Shultz on the plan: Israel would sell U.S.-made TOW missiles to Iran, and the United States would sell Israel more missiles to replace them. Shultz and Weinberger were still against selling arms directly to Iran.

Before the end of the month, the president had approved the plan. On August 20, Israel delivered 96 TOW missiles to Iran, followed by 408 more

A SHADY CHARACTER

Manucher Ghorbanifar played a large role in the arms-for-hostages side of the Iran-Contra affair. He was a shady and somewhat mysterious man who made many dramatic claims about his history. He said that he once had been an officer in the Iranian army, that he had worked for the SAVAK, and that he still had contacts at high levels in the Iranian government. No one could determine whether these claims were true. What was well known to the Americans was that Ghorbanifar had been an informant for the CIA from 1980 to 1982. The agency had decided he was unreliable. As a result, it had put him on a "burn list" of individuals with whom the agency should not associate. Still, the Israelis trusted him enough to involve him in the arms-for-hostages deal. And the Israelis convinced the Americans to trust him, too.

59

TOW missiles on September 14. On September 15, Hezbollah released one hostage, a Presbyterian minister named Benjamin Weir. Five more remained in custody. The Americans did not know it at the time, but one of the hostages, CIA Beirut station chief William Buckley, had died of untreated pneumonia on June 3.

Five days after his release, the Reverend Benjamin Weir and his wife, Carol, appeared at a press conference.

At several meetings in September and October, Ghorbanifar gave U.S. officials a list of more missiles the Iranians wanted: anti-aircraft HAWKs, Sidewinders, Harpoons, and Phoenix missiles.

U.S. and Israeli officials negotiated the delivery of these additional weapons to Iran and their replacement to Israel by the United States. President Reagan approved the plan, and McFarlane instructed Oliver North to oversee the deal. McFarlane told the secretary of state that another load of arms soon would be shipped to Iran. He also informed Vice President Bush.

North enlisted Secord's help to arrange the shipping details. To keep Israel's involvement in the shipment secret, the plan was to use three planes to fly 80 HAWK missiles from Israel to Lisbon, Portugal, on November 22. Then the missiles would be transferred to other planes that would take them to Iran. Before each shipment of missiles arrived in Iran, hostages were to be released in Beirut.

But the shipment went wrong from the start. North and Secord could not get the necessary clearances from the Portuguese government to land in Lisbon. They lost the opportunity to use the planes originally arranged for and instead arranged for a CIA-owned plane to fly from Germany to Tel Aviv, Israel, to pick up the missiles. But only 18 HAWK missiles would fit on the plane.

The plane landed in Tehran on November 25. When the Iranians saw what they had received, they were furious. The Iranians had paid for 80 new HAWK missiles in advance. There were only 18 missiles, and they were old models with the Star of David—the symbol of Israel—on them.

The failed shipment caused other problems, too. Not only was a CIA-owned airplane used, but the CIA also had become involved in trying to negotiate landing permission from Portugal. All these activities were secret actions. Therefore, according to a 1974 law, these actions needed to be officially approved by the president in advance by means of a finding. President Reagan signed such a finding on December 5, 1985, 10 days after the actions took place. The finding said that everything the CIA had done was part of a plan to trade arms for hostages and that the plan was approved by the president.

Everyone involved in the dealings—except Weinberger and Shultz—continued to support the arms deals. President Reagan signed a new finding on January 6, 1986. It authorized continued secret arms sales through Israel. The purpose of the arms sales, it said, was to achieve the release of hostages and improve relations with Iran. On January 17, at Casey's suggestion, the president signed yet another finding that authorized the use of third parties— namely Secord—to transfer the weapons. This would, the administration believed, allow them to bypass approval from Congress and distance the administration from the operation.

On February 18, an Israeli plane delivered 500 missiles to Iran. On February 27, 500 more were delivered. The Enterprise had paid $3.7 million for the missiles to the CIA, which had bought them from the U.S. Army. The Enterprise then sold

~~~ of te~~ism. You have discussed the general
outlines of the Israeli plan with Secretaries Shultz and
Weinberger, Attorney General Meese and Director Casey. The
Secretaries do not recommend you proceed with this plan.
Attorney General Meese and Director Casey believe the short-term
and long-term objectives of the plan warrant the policy risks
involved and recommend you approve the attached Finding. Because
of the extreme sensitivity of this project, it is recommended
that you exercise your statutory prerogative to withhold
notification of the Finding to the Congressional oversight
committees until such time that you deem it to be appropriate.

Recommendation

OK **NO**

RR __   That you sign the attached Finding.

                              Prepared by:
                              Oliver L. North

Attachment
    Tab A - Covert Action Finding   *1000 17 Jan 8.*

President was briefed verbally from this paper
VP, Don Regan and Don Fortier were present.

them to Ghorbanifar for $10 million. Ghorbanifar increased the price and sold them to the Iranians. The Enterprise still had $800,000 remaining from a $1 million payment from Israel for the November 1985 shipment.

President Reagan signed a finding on January 17, 1986, that authorized Richard Secord to secretly transfer weapons to Iran.

Around this time a new scheme was forming, but when, where, and how it was born is unclear. North was devising ways to use the profits from the arms sales to fund the Contras. By April 1986, the plan was complete enough that North could present it

63

Robert McFarlane (left) announced his resignation from the post of national security adviser in December 1985. His replacement, John Poindexter (right), and President Reagan joined him as he made his statement to reporters.

to his superiors. In a memo to President Reagan and John Poindexter (who had replaced McFarlane as national security adviser), North outlined how profits from the arms sales could be diverted, or sent, to the Contras. This memo, titled "Release of the American Hostages in Beirut," became known as the "diversion memo." Part of the $6.3 million profit from the February arms sales was diverted to the Enterprise to use on behalf of the Contras. North also decided to give the Enterprise the $800,000 from the November 1985 shipment.

But the main aim of the February arms shipments did not happen—Hezbollah failed to release even one hostage. In a series of meetings in March, April, and May 1986, Ghorbanifar, North, and other U.S. officials discussed a new plan. In exchange for a shipment of spare parts for HAWK missiles, Iran would arrange the release of the rest of the hostages.

They planned for a group of Americans, including McFarlane and North, to personally deliver the spare parts to Iran. McFarlane had resigned as national security adviser in December, but he remained involved in the operation. While there, the American agents, according to Ghorbanifar, would meet with high-level Iranian officials, and the rest of the American hostages would be released immediately.

North, McFarlane, and the others landed in Tehran on May 25 with a shipment of spare parts. During three days of talks it became more and more clear that the Iranians they were dealing with had no real power to force the release of all the hostages. The best they could offer was the possibility that

TRIP TO TEHRAN

The trip the American agents took to Tehran was nearly a disaster. The agents flew to Tehran in an Israeli plane disguised to look like a plane from another country. The crew had false flight plans, and the agents carried fake Irish passports. They brought gifts for the Iranians, including a chocolate cake. The cake was a particularly insensitive gift because the visit took place during Ramadan, the holy month in which devout Muslims do not eat from sunrise to sunset. When the agents arrived in Tehran, security guards took away the missile parts, the gifts, and their passports. The Americans were taken to the top floor of a luxury hotel and were nearly arrested by members of Iran's Revolutionary Guard. But they were saved when other Iranians fought the Guards off in the hotel parking lot.

65

one or perhaps two hostages would be released. Yet the Iranians continued to demand more weapons and parts. Humiliated and defeated, the Americans returned home.

Relations with the Iranians took a blow when the Iranians got their hands on an official Department of Defense price list for HAWK spare parts. They were angry to learn that North had slapped a steep markup on the price he charged them.

On July 26, hostage the Reverend Lawrence Jenco, a Catholic priest, was released. Two days later, at a meeting in Frankfurt, Germany, Ghorbanifar said that he, his Iranian contact, and an American hostage would be executed unless more parts were delivered. North recommended that the Iranian demand be met, and President Reagan approved it. The parts were delivered on August 3 and 4, 1986.

Though negotiations for the release of the hostages continued, the entire operation would soon crumble. First, two more Americans were kidnapped in Beirut. Frank Reed was taken on September 9 and Joseph Cicippio on September 12. The tally was now two hostages released, and two more kidnapped to replace them.

Then on October 6, the Sandinistas shot down a CIA supply plane over Nicaragua. Details of the diversion of arms sales profits to fund the Contras had begun to leak to U.S. officials, including CIA Director Casey.

American Hostages Taken in Lebanon, 1984–1986

Hostage	Date Kidnapped	What Happened
Jeremy Levin, Beirut chief for Cable News Network (CNN)	March 7, 1984	escaped February 14, 1985
The Reverend Benjamin Weir, Presbyterian minister	May 8, 1984	released September 15, 1985
William Buckley, CIA Beirut station chief	March 16, 1984	died in custody June 3, 1986
The Reverend Lawrence Jenco, senior official with Catholic Relief Services in Beirut	January 8, 1985	released July 26, 1986
Terry Anderson, chief Middle East correspondent for the Associated Press	May 16, 1985	released December 4, 1991
David Jacobsen, director of American University Hospital in Beirut	May 28, 1985	released November 2, 1986
Thomas Sutherland, dean of agriculture, University of Beirut	June 9, 1985	released November 18, 1991
Frank Reed, director of American University in Beirut	September 9, 1986	released April 30, 1990
Joseph Cicippio, controller of American University in Beirut	September 12, 1986	released December 2, 1991

At the end of October, the United States delivered 500 more missiles, for which Iran paid $3.6 million. The kidnappers released hostage David Jacobsen. He would be the last hostage released as a result of arms sales. ◣

The Secret Gets Out

Chapter

7

On November 3, a magazine in Lebanon called *Al-Shiraa* published an account of North and McFarlane's visit to Tehran. North, McFarlane, Casey, and the others remained tight-lipped in response to the story. According to a North aide, they all agreed to say nothing. When they absolutely had to say something, they would tell a "very carefully crafted artful truth, where possible or necessary, or if there is no other way, outright denial." But those involved in the operation could not keep quiet for long.

The story of U.S. arms sales caused a sensation around the world. The idea that the Reagan administration would secretly go against the policies that it trumpeted—no arms sales to Iran, no dealing with terrorists—damaged the government's reputation. Those involved in the operation quickly went to work to devise a version of events—a "carefully crafted artful truth"—in which no unauthorized arms sales had taken place.

The first person in the line of fire was, ironically, George Shultz. As secretary of state, Shultz should have been second only to the president in the conduct of foreign policy. But after Shultz's repeated objections to the idea of selling arms to Iran, others in the Reagan administration had kept him in the dark. McFarlane had given Shultz notice of the ill-fated November 1985 arms shipment, but Shultz knew nothing about the 1986 shipments.

At a press conference on November 4, 1986, Shultz was bombarded with questions about the November 1985 arms sale. His only comment was

George Shultz served as President Reagan's secretary of state. He opposed all activities aimed at arming the Contras and trading weapons for hostages.

that any questions about arms sales to Iran should be directed at the White House. He dashed off a note to National Security Adviser Poindexter expressing his concern that the story would continue to grow unless the administration put out a statement. He suggested that the president tell the public that the 1986 shipment was:

> *a special, one-time operation based on humanitarian grounds and decided by the president within his constitutional responsibility to act in the service of national interest.*

What Shultz did not know was just how far from "special" and "one-time" the operation was.

A meeting was called for November 10 in the White House to decide what to tell the public. President Reagan, Vice President Bush, Secretary of State Shultz, Secretary of Defense Weinberger, White House Chief of Staff Donald Regan, National Security Adviser Poindexter, and Attorney General Edwin Meese were there. Despite the fact that he had given authorization in the form of written findings, the president stated several times that the administration had never traded arms for hostages or dealt with terrorists. Now he appeared to believe his version of events.

Under increasing pressure from the media, the president decided to address the American people in a televised speech on November 13. The day before the speech, the president wrote in his diary:

PLAYERS IN THE IRAN-CONTRA AFFAIR

Name	Title	Job Description
Ronald Reagan	President of the United States	Chief executive of the United States
George H.W. Bush	Vice President of the United States	Second-highest executive of the United States
George Shultz	Secretary of State	Adviser to the president on foreign affairs
Caspar Weinberger	Secretary of Defense	Adviser to the president on military matters, including defense, weapons, and intelligence
Edwin Meese	Attorney General	Head of the Department of Justice and chief law-enforcement officer of the United States
Robert McFarlane (later John Poindexter)	National Security Adviser	Adviser to the president on national-security issues, especially foreign relations and military matters
Donald Regan	White House Chief of Staff	Chief assistant to the president; manages the president's schedule and the White House staff
William Casey	Director of Central Intelligence	Head of the Central Intelligence Agency
Abraham Sofaer	State Department legal adviser	Advises secretary of state on legal matters

> *This whole irresponsible press bilge about hostages and Iran has gotten totally out of hand. ... I want to go public personally and tell the people the truth.*

In his speech, the president said that the arms shipments, all together, were small enough to "fit into a single cargo plane." He said that "all appropriate Cabinet members were fully consulted" on the operation, and that the U.S. government did not trade weapons for hostages. The public was skeptical. Polls showed that only 14 percent of Americans believed the president's statements.

On November 19, the president again faced the nation, this time at a press conference. He showed a lack of understanding of the facts. He did not know exactly what TOW missiles were. He said, "We did not condone and do not condone the shipment of arms from other countries." When reporters pointed out that his chief of staff, Donald Regan, had said that the administration had approved the shipment of weapons from Israel to Iran in September 1985, the president simply replied that he did not know Regan had said that and that he would ask him about it.

The congressional committees that oversaw intelligence activities requested that Poindexter and North appear for a hearing. The two men stated that they had authorized the use of a CIA plane to deliver cargo from Israel to Iran in November 1985. But now they were claiming they thought the cargo was made up of parts for oil drilling equipment, not missiles.

The same day, the legal adviser for the State Department, Abraham Sofaer, learned about a conversation in November 1985—12 months earlier—in which McFarlane had told Shultz that missiles were to be shipped to Iran in exchange for hostages. Moments later, a CIA official arrived with a copy of the testimony Casey planned to give at the congressional hearings the next day. Casey's planned testimony was that the CIA plane that landed in Iran had been loaded with oil drilling equipment. When Sofaer read this, he knew Casey was planning to lie. Sofaer later said:

> *I was not assuming that anything that had been done was illegal. What I knew was that a cover-up was illegal and whatever you might be able to say about the legality of something you did, there is no way you could claim that a cover-up is legal.*

The news of Casey's planned testimony was reported to Meese later that night. It was then that he realized that a deception was taking place.

Meese met with President Reagan, Poindexter, and Regan and suggested that he be allowed to put

President Reagan (right) discussed the situation with (from left) Caspar Weinberger, George Shultz, Edwin Meese, and Donald Regan in the Oval Office.

together a summary of the facts of the operation. The president agreed. He asked Meese to complete the summary in three days so that it would be ready for a meeting of the National Security Planning Group scheduled for November 24.

Meese told Poindexter that he would be sending aides to his office to collect documents relevant to the case. In the presence of North and an NSC lawyer, Poindexter tore up the original finding that President Reagan had signed on December 5, 1985. This had approved—after the fact—the sale of HAWK missiles to Iran in exchange for hostages. After the president and all involved had denied knowledge of this shipment, the finding was a bombshell waiting to explode. Poindexter justified destroying it by saying that it would be "politically embarrassing" for the president.

North and his secretary, Fawn Hall, had been destroying records since earlier that month. Now they continued with more urgency. They shredded memos and phone records and altered documents. North deleted 736 computer messages from a special private channel in the National Security Council computer system that he and Poindexter used to communicate with each other.

One document that escaped the shredder was a draft of the diversion memo. Meese's aides found it in North's office on November 22. The diversion memo was clear evidence that laws had been broken. The arms sales violated the National

Security Act, which says that certain House and Senate committees must be informed of secret activities by the CIA. They also violated the Arms Export Control Act, which outlines requirements for the legal selling of weapons to foreign governments. Specifically it prohibits the export of U.S. arms to a country via a third country. The money that North had diverted to the Contras belonged to the U.S. government. Only Congress can decide how government funds are spent, so the diversion was essentially theft. The memo was another smoking gun that could implicate

"CLEANING THINGS UP"

After the Enterprise's Southern Air Transport plane was shot down in Nicaragua, Oliver North and the other players in Iran-Contra knew they had to start covering their tracks. North began to shred documents in his office. Casey told him that a ledger book that North had kept throughout the operation was especially sensitive. The book had the names and addresses of everyone who had been paid to provide help to the Contras. North destroyed the book on November 4 or 5. On November 21, North and his secretary, Fawn Hall, continued the cleanup. She testified later that she helped shred a pile of documents.

Fawn Hall typed changes that North made to documents to cover up the fact that his activities violated one of the Boland amendments. When North's office was sealed, Hall smuggled the documents from the White House.

75

the president. But North assured Meese that the memo had never gone to the president.

Reagan, Bush, Shultz, Weinberger, Regan, Casey, Poindexter, and Meese gathered for the National Security Planning Group meeting on November 24. Chief of Staff Regan asked who knew about the November 25, 1985, arms shipment. He wanted to know who approved it and whether the president knew about it. Poindexter pointed the finger at McFarlane. The president said nothing in answer to Regan's questions. Everyone seemed content to protect the president by blaming the entire scheme on McFarlane. Meese did not bring up the diversion memo.

Later in the day, Meese and Regan told the president about the diversion of arms profits to the Contras. Meese later recalled that the president had reacted calmly. The three men discussed Poindexter's role. Poindexter had told Meese that he had known about the diversion of funds but had done nothing to stop Oliver North. The next morning, Meese asked Poindexter to resign.

President Reagan held a press conference the next day, November 25, 1986. He told the version of the story that his aides had been devising during the previous weeks. He said that he had not been fully informed of the details of the activities. He announced the resignation of John Poindexter and said that Oliver North had been "relieved of his duties." He left without answering questions.

Attorney General Meese then stepped up to the podium. He said that Israel had been responsible for the arms sales to Iran and that it was the Israelis who had deposited the money into a Swiss bank account for the Contras. He said, again, that the president had not learned about the November 1985 missile shipment until months later. He blamed those who carried out the operation for keeping the president in the dark.

Edwin Meese (left) echoed Reagan's speech by saying that the president was unaware of the secret operations.

Soon, however, Congress and the court system would go to work to find out the truth. Although the true story of the illegal dealings would slowly emerge, only six people involved in the affair—and none of the major players—would ever be punished. ◣

Called to Account

Chapter

8

As the details of the Iran-Contra affair came to light in November and early December 1986, it was clear that the U.S. Congress and the American people had to be told the truth.

Three investigations were established:

•. The president ordered the formation of a bipartisan review board to look into the actions of the National Security Council.

• The House of Representatives and Senate set up select committees to investigate the Iran-Contra affair. They would hold joint hearings.

• The president ordered an independent judicial investigation headed by an independent counsel, whose job was to determine whether laws had been broken and to bring criminal charges if they had.

The bipartisan review board came to be known as the Tower Commission, after its chairman, John Tower, a former Republican senator from Texas. Former National Security Adviser Brent Scowcroft—a Republican—and former Secretary of State Edmund Muskie—a Democrat—assisted Tower. They worked to find out how the NSC operated during the Iran-Contra affair, as well as how it operated throughout its history to fulfill its overall mission.

The Tower Commission report criticized the NSC for ignoring the State Department, the Defense Department, and the CIA. The commission implied that it agreed with the idea that the president's aides had tried so hard to put forth—that President Reagan had not known about any improper or illegal activities. It laid much of the blame on National Security Adviser Poindexter.

The Tower Commission presented its report on the Iran-Contra affair on February 26, 1987. President Reagan introduced the members of the commission to the White House press corps.

In January 1987, the two congressional committees—one in the House and one in the Senate—joined to hold hearings on the Iran-Contra affair. The investigation was to focus on four main issues: arms sales to Iran, diversion of funds to the Contras, violations of federal law, and NSC involvement in foreign policy.

The committees completed their private preliminary investigations, and public televised testimony began on May 5, 1987. For the next three months, an estimated 55 million viewers per day were captivated by tales of secret operations—deals involving millions of dollars, secret meetings in exotic locations, guns, airplanes, missiles, and "freedom fighters" in the jungle.

Most of the major players testified. The first witness called was Richard Secord, who referred to himself as the general who had called all the shots. He told the committee how the Enterprise ran dummy corporations, held Swiss bank accounts, and acquired and operated numerous assets in its arms dealings for Iran and the Contras.

John Poindexter's testimony cast doubt on President Reagan's leadership. He testified that he never told the president that money from the arms sales had been diverted to the Contras. He justified the action by saying he was certain the president would have approved of it anyway. Poindexter, a brilliant man who had been first in his class at the U.S. Naval Academy, earned a Ph.D. in nuclear physics, and reportedly had a photographic memory, responded more than 180 times with "I don't remember" or "I can't recall."

Oliver North admitted he had lied to Congress, but much of the public seemed not to mind. People were impressed by this patriotic and handsome Marine who wore a uniform decorated with medals. North's approval ratings shot up, and so did public support for aid to the Contras. North skillfully justified the administration's reasons for undertaking the Iran-Contra operations.

The hearings ended August 3, 1987. In all, the committees conducted 41 days of testimony, heard from 28 public witnesses and about 500 more private witnesses, and reviewed 300,000 documents. On November 18, 1987, the committees issued their 1,200-page joint report.

Oliver North captured the nation's attention. He testified for six days in July under partial immunity from prosecution. This meant that what he told Congress could not be used against him in a criminal trial.

The conclusion of the report stated:

> *The common ingredients of the Iran and Contra policies were secrecy, deception, and disdain for the law. A small group of senior officials believed that they alone knew what was right. ... They told neither the Secretary of State, the Congress, nor the American people of their actions. When exposure was threatened, they destroyed official documents and lied to Cabinet officials, to the public, and the elected representatives in Congress. They testified that they even withheld key facts from the President.*

The report left many contradictions, loose ends, and unanswered questions. Because of the veil of secrecy, the destruction of many important documents, and the death of CIA Director William Casey before he could testify, many facts about the case will never be known.

Reporters picked up copies of the Iran-Contra report, but it failed to provide a full, understandable account of the affair.

While the congressional hearings were going on, the third independent investigation was going forward with a different purpose. This was a criminal investigation, ordered by the president. Lawrence E. Walsh, a 75-year-old former deputy attorney general who had returned to private law practice, was named independent counsel, or head of the investigation.

The independent counsel's main concern was to find out what crimes had been committed and to prosecute the guilty. As winter turned into spring, these tasks brought the independent counsel into conflict with Congress in some areas. Congress was eager to grant immunity from prosecution to certain witnesses—especially North and Poindexter—to encourage them to tell their full stories in public. Congress was in a hurry to begin the hearings because it wanted them over well before the presidential election season began the next year.

But the independent counsel wanted to bring charges against those who he believed had committed serious crimes. Grants of immunity made the independent counsel's job much harder. Any statement made during the congressional hearings by a witness testifying under immunity,

INDEPENDENT COUNSEL

An independent counsel has a unique role in the U.S. judicial system. This person is a lawyer in private practice who is chosen by a court to fulfill a legal task. The independent counsel fills the role of the attorney general when that official cannot perform that role. In the case of Iran-Contra, Attorney General Edwin Meese acted more as legal counsel to the president than as chief law enforcement officer of the land. The independent counsel essentially has to create an entire agency from scratch to carry out the investigation.

83

such as North and Poindexter, could not be used against him in a criminal trial.

During the next six years, the independent counsel investigated and got indictments, or brought charges against, 14 people involved in the Iran-Contra affair. Nine of these people were government officials, and five were private citizens. Of these, Richard Secord, Robert McFarlane, the businessman Albert Hakim, and four others pleaded guilty and were sentenced.

Caspar Weinberger and another individual received pardons from President George H.W. Bush on December 24, 1992, before they went to trial. McFarlane and four others who were found guilty also received pardons the same day. One person's case was dismissed on November 24, 1989, after the U.S. government refused to declassify, or make public, secret information needed for the case.

North, Poindexter, and two others stood trial and were convicted. Poindexter and North both were

A PRESIDENTIAL DUTY

The Iran-Contra investigations raised several constitutional and legal questions. President Reagan escaped criminal charges by denying any knowledge of illegal activities. According to the Constitution, though, the president is responsible for carrying out the laws of the country. But the president allowed appointed staff members to make decisions that affected important aspects of foreign policy and national security. Many people asked whether he had in this way shirked his constitutional duties.

convicted on several felony counts. However, their convictions were overturned on legal technicalities. The court decided that their convictions may have been unfair.

The Iran-Contra affair demonstrated a violation of the separation of powers. Each branch of the U.S. government operates in a way so no one branch can have too much power. Oliver North and the others secretly spent U.S. taxpayer money and formed agreements with foreign powers. But the Constitution says that these activities must be approved by Congress. The violation of the separation of powers and the breaking of laws by government officials shattered many Americans' trust in the government.

Senator Daniel Patrick Moynihan, a Democrat from New York, referred to the affair as a "massive ... hemorrhaging of trust and integrity." He condemned the actions of those involved with these strong words:

> *The very processes of American government were put in harm's way by a conspiracy of faithless or witless men: sometimes both.*

The strength of the U.S. Constitution and the freedom it gives for voices like those of Senator Moynihan to be heard helps ensure that although wrongdoers can sometimes bend the system, in the end, they cannot break it. ◪

Timeline

March 12, 1947
Truman Doctrine declared.

July 26, 1947
National Security Act creates National Security Council and Central Intelligence Agency.

February 1, 1979

Ayatollah Ruhollah Khomeini takes over government of Iran after Islamic revolution.

July 17, 1979
Sandinistas take control of Nicaragua.

November 17, 1981
President Ronald Reagan authorizes secret aid to Contras.

December 8, 1983
First Boland amendment prohibits aid to Contras.

Spring or summer 1984
President Reagan directs National Security Adviser Robert McFarlane to keep the Contras together "body and soul."

March 1984–June 1985
Shiite terrorists kidnap seven U.S. citizens in Beirut, Lebanon.

June 16, 1985
Reagan declares that the United States will never deal with terrorists.

July 18, 1985

McFarlane first proposes trading arms for hostages to President Reagan.

August 20, 1985
Ninety-six anti-tank, or TOW, missiles shipped to Iran.

September 14, 1985
Four hundred eight TOW missiles shipped to Iran.

September 15, 1985
Hostage Benjamin Weir released.

November 25, 1985
Eighteen HAWK missiles delivered to Iran.

December 5, 1985
Reagan signs finding authorizing November arms shipment to Iran.

January 6, 1986
Reagan signs second finding authorizing arms shipments to Iran.

January 17, 1986
Reagan signs third finding authorizing shipping arms to Iran through third parties.

February 18, 1986
Five hundred TOW missiles shipped to Iran.

February 27, 1986
Another shipment of 500 TOW missiles delivered to Iran.

May 25, 1986
McFarlane leads delegation to Iran to deliver missile parts and negotiate for release of hostages.

July 26, 1986
Hostage Lawrence Jenco released.

August 3–4, 1986
Spare parts for HAWK missiles shipped to Iran.

September 9, 1986
American Frank Reed taken hostage in Beirut.

September 12, 1986
American Joseph Cicippio taken hostage in Beirut.

October 6, 1986

American plane carrying supplies for Contras shot down over Nicaragua.

October 28, 1986
Five hundred TOW missiles shipped to Iran.

November 2, 1986
Hostage David Jacobsen is released.

November 3, 1986
Lebanese magazine *Al-Shiraa* publishes story about arms-for-hostages deal.

November 4, 1986

George Shultz deflects questions about Iran-Contra at a press conference.

November 13, 1986
Reagan publicly denies trading arms for hostages.

November 19, 1986
At a press conference, Reagan contradicts earlier statements.

November 22, 1986
Memo detailing plans for diversion of funds from arms sales to Contras is discovered in North's office.

November 25, 1986
Reagan and Attorney General Edwin Meese hold press conference during which they claim that Israel sold the weapons and delivered the profits.

December 1, 1986
Reagan appoints Tower Commission.

December 19, 1986
Lawrence Walsh is sworn in as independent counsel.

Timeline

January 6, 1987

Senate forms committee to investigate Iran-Contra affair.

January 7, 1987

House forms committee to investigate Iran-Contra affair.

February 26, 1987

 Tower Commission releases report.

March 3, 1987

Reagan apologizes for trading arms for hostages in a speech to the American people.

May 5–August 3, 1987

Congressional hearings are held.

November 18, 1987

Congress releases its report on Iran-Contra affair.

March 11, 1988

McFarlane pleads guilty to four misdemeanor counts related to Iran-Contra affair.

May 4, 1989

 Oliver North convicted of three felonies related to Iran-Contra affair.

November 8, 1989

Richard Secord pleads guilty to one felony related to Iran-Contra affair.

April 7, 1990

John Poindexter convicted of five felonies related to Iran-Contra affair.

June 16 and October 30, 1992

Caspar Weinberger indicted on charges related to Iran-Contra affair; pardoned before he goes to trial.

December 24, 1992

President George H.W. Bush pardons Weinberger, McFarlane, Elliott Abrams, Dewey R. (Duane) Clarridge, Alan Fiers, and Clair George for all crimes they may have committed related to the Iran-Contra affair.

On the Web

For more information on this topic, use FactHound.

1 Go to *www.facthound.com*

2 Type in this book ID: 0756534801

3 Click on the *Fetch It!* button. FactHound will find the best Web sites for you.

Historic Sites

The Ronald Reagan Presidential Library and Museum
40 Presidential Drive
Simi Valley, CA 93065
800/410-8354

The library and museum contain documents, images, and other items from Reagan's time in office.

The George Bush Presidential Library and Museum
1000 George Bush Drive West
College Station, TX 77845
979/691-4000

Includes information on President Bush's pardon of Caspar Weinberger and background material on Iran-Contra.

Look for More Books in This Series

Black Tuesday:
Prelude to the Great Depression

The Berlin Airlift:
Breaking the Soviet Blockade

The Cultural Revolution:
Years of Chaos in China

A Day Without Immigrants:
Rallying Behind America's Newcomers

Kristallnacht, The Night of Broken Glass:
Igniting the Nazi War Against Jews

A complete list of **Snapshots in History** titles is available on our Web site: *www.compasspointbooks.com*

Glossary

bipartisan
made up of members of both the
Republican and Democratic parties

Cabinet
president's group of advisers who are
heads of government agencies

communism
political system in which goods and
property are owned by the government
and shared in common

Contras
rebels who opposed the Sandinista
government in Nicaragua

embargo
official refusal to buy or sell goods to
another country as a form of protest

**Frente Sandinista de
Liberación Nacional**
(Sandinista Revolutionary Front) Contra
group made up of disgruntled Sandinistas
based in Costa Rica

Fuerza Democrática Nicaragüense
(Nicaraguan Democratic Force) Contra
group made up of former officers of the
Nicaraguan National Guard who were
based in Honduras

indict
charge with a crime

intelligence
information secretly gathered by spies or
electronic devices

National Security Council
group within the executive branch of
government that advises the president on
national security

Sandinistas
rebel group in Nicaragua formed in 1961
to oppose the Somoza regime

scandal
disgraceful or shameful action

secular
concerned with matters that are
worldly or practical, rather than
spiritual or religious

select committee
temporary group in Congress formed for
a special purpose, such as an investigation

shah
the monarch, or king, in Iran

Swiss bank account
an account in a Swiss bank; the Swiss
banking system is one of the world's most
secretive, and there is no way to find out
who owns a Swiss bank account nor the
source of money deposited in it

TOW missile
missile launched from a tripod, vehicle,
or helicopter, used to destroy tanks;
stands for "tube-launched, optically
guided, wire-controlled"

Source Notes

Chapter 1
Page 11, line 4: Theodore Draper. *A Very Thin Line: The Iran-Contra Affairs.* New York: Hill & Wang, 1991, p. 353.

Page 12, sidebar line 3: Stewart Powell. "Whose war is it? Nobody owns up." *U.S. News & World Report,* 3 Nov. 1986, p. 35.

Page 12, sidebar line 8: Brian Duffy. "The Chilly Money Trail." *U.S. News & World Report,* 29 Dec. 1986, p. 6.

Page 13, line 8: "Reagan Denies U.S. Link to Plane." *Chicago Tribune.* 9 Oct. 1986, natl. ed., p. 1.

Page 13, line 22: "Reagan Quotes." *The American Experience.* PBS Online. 18 Sept. 2007, www.pbs.org/wgbh/amex/reagan/sfeature/quotes.html

Chapter 2
Page 18, line 28: "Truman Doctrine." The Avalon Project. 18 Sept. 2007, www.yale.edu/lawweb/avalon/trudoc.htm

Page 23, line 17: James E. Gauch. *Restoring Congress's Proper Role in Oversight of Covert Intelligence Operations.* The Federalist Society for Law and Public Policy Studies. 19 Sept. 2007, www.fed-soc.org/doclib/20070326_CIA.pdf

Chapter 4
Page 39, line 14: "Uncle Sam as Destabilizer." Editorial. *Boston Globe.* 5 Nov. 1982.

Page 40, line 3: *A Very Thin Line: The Iran-Contra Affairs,* p. 18.

Page 41, line 5: Ibid., p. 27.

Page 42, line 6: Ibid., pp. 20–21.

Chapter 5
Page 48, lines 8 and 10: Lawrence E. Walsh. *Final Report of the Independent Counsel for Iran/Contra Matters.* Vol. 1. 1993. 18 Sept. 2007. www.fas.org/irp/offdocs/walsh/chap_01.htm

Page 49, line 6: Ibid.

Source Notes

Chapter 6

Page 57, line 10: "Ronald Reagan, The President's News Conference." June 18th, 1985. *The American Presidency Project.* 18 Sept. 2007, www.presidency.ucsb.edu/ws/print.php?pid=38789

Chapter 7

Page 68, line 8: *A Very Thin Line: The Iran-Contra Affairs,* p. 459.

Page 70, line 8: Ibid., p. 463.

Page 71, line 1: Lawrence E. Walsh. *Firewall: The Iran-Contra Conspiracy and Cover-Up.* New York: Norton, 1998, pp. 9–10.

Page 71, line 7: *A Very Thin Line: The Iran-Contra Affairs,* p. 474.

Page 72, line 9: Ibid., p. 482.

Page 73, line 8: Ibid., p. 491.

Page 74, line 17: Ibid., p. 501.

Page 76, line 29: Ibid., p. 528.

Chapter 8

Page 81, line 2: Brian Duffy. "A troubling midsummer mystery." *U.S. News & World Report,* 10 Aug. 1987, p. 14.

Page 82, line 2: Daniel K. Inouye and Lee H. Hamilton. *Report of the Congressional Committees Investigating the Iran-Contra Affair.* Abridged ed. New York: Random House, 1988, p. 21.

Page 85, lines 18 and 21: *A Very Thin Line: The Iran-Contra Affairs,* p. 22.

SELECT BIBLIOGRAPHY

Draper, Theodore. *A Very Thin Line: The Iran-Contra Affairs.* New York: Hill and Wang, 1991.

Inouye, Daniel K., and Lee H. Hamilton. *Report of the Congressional Committees Investigating the Iran-Contra Affair.* Abridged ed. New York: Random House, 1988.

Walsh, Lawrence E. *Firewall: The Iran-Contra Conspiracy and Cover-Up.* New York: Norton, 1998.

FURTHER READING

Johnson, Darv. *The Reagan Years.* San Diego, Calif.: Lucent Books, 2000.

Keeley, Jennifer. *Containing the Communists: America's Foreign Entanglements.* San Diego, Calif.: Lucent Books, 2003.

Lawson, Don. *America Held Hostage: The Iran Hostage Crisis and the Iran-Contra Affair.* New York: Franklin Watts, 1991.

Petersen, Christine. *The Iran-Contra Scandal.* New York: Children's Press, 2004.

Index

ABOUT THE AUTHOR

Lisa Klobuchar is the author of more than 25 nonfiction books and dozens of articles for young people. A native of northwestern Indiana, she lives in Chicago.

IMAGE CREDITS